MW01127793

Study to Study

By
Elder Elton Cottrell, Sr.
&
Anna Godwin, Ph.D

Study to Study

By
Elder Elton Cottrell, Sr.
&
Anna Godwin, Ph.D

Copyright © 2010
All Rights Reserved

PUBLISHED BY:
BRENTWOOD CHRISTIAN PRESS
COLUMBUS, GEORGIA 31904
WWW.BRENTWOODBOOKS.COM

DEDICATION

This book is dedicated to this generation and to the ones to come who are hungry and thirsty after righteousness. To our grandchildren, Jordan, Brooke, Elyse, Caleb, Kammeryn, Keyvion, and Kayden; to our lovely, dearest sons and daughters of the Gospel, Ashley, Keith, Wayne, and Anton, we wanted to leave a heritage to you about life. Remember this principle: Study to Study. When faced with life's challenges study to find your answers. Study the ways of evil men. You should study to show yourself approved unto God and study to be quiet. A workman need not be ashamed, rightly dividing the word of truth. Always remember, when people show you their real self, believe them. Above all else, love the Lord your God with all of your heart, mind, body and soul. We love you all so much. We wait anxiously for your coming after.

Grandma Anna and Papaw

CONTENTS

ACKNOWLEDGEMENTS

We are truly thankful for God Almighty for his favor, mercy, grace, inspiration, guidance for keeping us on track to complete this project. Where would we be without our Lord and Savior? Thanks for choosing us to pen with the anointing ways to teach a global society during a time of recession.

To the late, Mr. Elliot Cottrell, Sr., Mrs. Annie B. Spears-Cottrell, Mr. Louis T. Stanback, and Mrs. Eularia Marie Hill and friends who supported us in this endeavor. We love you for your endless and tireless prayers and encouragement.

Mrs. Sylvia Akins, Ms. Yalunda Johnson, and Ms. Rugena Bivins, thanks for being the best editors, eyes of inspiration, enlightenment, enhancement, and truthfulness.

To all Pastors, Ministries of our past, present, and future, we recognize your labor of love and we say, "Thank you for your impartations." To the late Dr. Alfred Hill and Reverend Henry Ward of Pilgrim Rest Missionary Baptist Church, Memphis, Tennessee; Mr. O. C. Collins, Sr, Progressive Baptist Church, Memphis, Tennessee; Bishop Charles and Marilyn Lanier, Faith Deliverance Church, Washington D.C.; Pastors Dr. Charles E. and Dora Wallace of Faith Deliverance Center, Jackson, Tennessee; Pastors Val and Sherry Treece, Family Worship Center, Jackson, Tennessee; God Parents, Pastors Walter and Clara Brewer, West Bemis Baptist Church, Jackson Tennessee; Pastor Dr. Charles H. Clark, Progressive Baptist Church, Jackson,

Tennessee; Pastor Dr. Stacey Spencer, New Direction Church, Memphis, Tennessee; Apostle Tina Edwards, Kingdom Men and Women of Destiny International Ministry, Memphis, Tennessee. Thank you for being a part of our first beginnings. Assuredly, the best is yet to come. We humbly appreciate the impact and influence of your labor of love, prayers and support toward us. Our prayer is that God will continue to bless you tremendously.

INTRODUCTION

"Have not I written to thee excellent things in counsels and knowledge, that I might make thee know the certainty of the words of truth; that thou mightest answer the words of truth to them that send unto thee?" (Proverbs 22:20-21).

The world is full of uncertainties, but God is for sure. There is safety and soundness for those who study and obey the word of the Lord. Know that a person who doesn't study the scriptures becomes an imposter to the faith. Perhaps this is why we fail so successfully. Those who don't study leave themselves at the mercies of others, becoming the perfect target or prey for predators who feed off the lusts and weaknesses of men. *"For among my people are found wicked men: they lay wait, as he that setteth snares; they set a trap, they catch me"* (Jeremiah 5:26). People who do not study become live bait and dead weight. It's been said that we live in the age of information. The world is so impressed with how smart and clever we are. *"And the Lord commended the unjust steward, because he had done wisely: for the children of this world are in their generation wiser than the children of light" (Luke 16:8). "Ever learning, and never able to come to the knowledge of the truth" (II Timothy*

3:7). It is written: "My people are destroyed for lack of knowledge: because thou has rejected knowledge, I will also reject thee, that thou shalt be no priest to me; seeing thou hast forgotten the law of thy God, I will also forget thy children"(Hosea 4:6). These studies are not designed to determine how intelligent you are, but to glorify how intelligent and great our creator is. It is to prepare you for the work at hand which is most needed for the harvest is ready, but the labors are few. *"Prepare thy work without, and make it fit for thyself in the field; and afterwards build thy house" (Proverbs 24:27).* Proper preparation prevents poor performance.

While we study various subject matter, somehow, some way, these studies and directives designed to increase human levels of consciousness have been neglected. These particular studies are designed to train, equip, and prepare us to process and filter information so we can discern between that which is right or wrong and good or evil. The untrained eyes, ears, and mouth are the perfect condition for ideas to infiltrate, inflict pain, or damage the body of Christ. Much of what we do and say goes without being challenged, questioned, or proven. *"So teach us to number our days, that we may apply our hearts unto wisdom" (Psalm 90:12).* Wisdom establishes our true level of consciousness. Therefore, be ye transformed by the renewing of your mind. Many of us who are conformed to this world undermine the true purpose of our existence. It's been stated, that the first casualty of war is the truth. *"And because I tell you the truth, ye believe me not" (John 8:45).*

On any given Sunday two football teams come together to test their skills against each other. They have practiced being hit and tackled. They put in motion their and defensive and offensive plays to prevent one another from scoring. They run, jump, and exercise to train their mind, body, spirit, and soul for a sport whose motive is to win and get paid on a professional level. These modern day gladiators are trained to put on their armor to protect them from injuries. Their love and passion for the game is displayed in their commitment, devotion, and dedication. While we sit in the stands amazed at their size, brutal strength, and talents. They are on the field experiencing the pain, and suffering the agony of disappointments. They suffer errors, penalties, losses, interceptions, and fumbles, but they also equally enjoy the moments of victory. Their focus is on getting the job done. It is written: *"Whatsoever thy hand findeth to do, do it with thy might; for there is no work, nor device, nor knowledge, nor wisdom, in the grave, whither thou goest"* *(Ecclesiastes 9:10).* For the football player behind the scenes, out of the public view, in secret, he comes face to face with the weakness and strength of his own humanity. Where it is not about how fast you can run, how well you can catch, or how well you can carry a football. The fear of being exposed, rejected, and despised for not being able to live up to the super hero image that has been superficially bestowed upon him. Because the reality of the matter is that if you take his football away from him, all of his dreams, hope, self worth, dignity, and identity are gone. Often, a man or a woman who loses their job, for whatever reason, feels despair, helplessness, hopelessness, worries, and depression over takes them.

Many are called, but few are chosen for these various reasons. The work we have been specifically assigned to perform has been replaced with a higher calling by man. Our love for money, the root of all evil, has changed the way we see God and man. The value of a human being has been reduced to the size of a coin or a paper dollar bill. We are driven by an artificial belief system that values a person by the size of his wallet and not the quality of his wisdom. The first study reveals the true motives, and intention of evil men. The next three will deal with the preparation for war. *"Suppose ye that I am come to give peace on earth? I tell you, Nay, but rather division:"(Luke 12:51).*

These four studies and four directives are designed to serve, to guide, or influence the power or consciousness of our being. Let us walk in the spirit and not fulfill the lust of the flesh.

The following studies and directives are four topics that God teaches us to observe in life. We will focus on one evil observation and three good observations. These studies have the ability to shape our character, reputation and personality if we so determine and apply them. They are also designed to prevent us from losing our eternal value from passing from one generation to others the true meaning of life. Lastly, they are the perfect cure for anti-social behavior.

Nevertheless, these studies have become obsolete, so have we. Therefore, we have become intimidated by God's presence, ashamed of his glory and have no respect for his honor. The world that we are born into is doomed for destruction. We can believe it because God has spoken. God's number one priority and agenda is to keep his word, his covenant with his people. Ours should be likewise. The reality of these studies and directives is that without them there is no reality. For we have this treasure in earthen vessels, that the excellence of power may be of God, and not of man.

If we fail to study: we study to fail. These studies create a true balance between God and man. *"Be ye not unequally yoked together with unbelievers: for what fellowship hath righteousness with unrighteousness? And what communion hath light with darkness?"(II Corinthians 6:14).* Scientist, doctors, lawyers, teachers and ministers do it to become skilled and proficient, and confident in their vocation. Kings and presidents surround themselves with such men and women. Those who study the issues commanded by God will be able to answer Kings and Presidents as well as surround themselves with the presence and authority of such men and women. Those who study these studies will become familiar with the tactics, strategies, and plans of evil men. Who respect and seek God's will, power, and purpose will become the head and not the tail. Who is quiet enough to wait and to hear the voice of God becomes the light of the world.

These four studies and directives hold the key to an unfaithful, unfruitful lifestyle. For we all have an important role to play in the growth and development of mankind. We are to ensure peace through a common denominator, belief, and truth of righteousness in God and him alone. If we expect to be the masters of the universe, we can no longer be the fools of Satan and the servants of sin. An unholy alliance with the forces of darkness. This is our fight, for lost souls. Mankind has been so demoralized, degraded, debased, dehumanized, until he sees no value in himself nor others. These four studies are our wisdom, knowledge and understanding, true weapons of war. We shall never forget our ancestors, and love for you, God. Because of them we know you. For if there be any restitution, that God will remain the foundation of our constitution.

For we will no longer be threaten by those who refuse to believe, and they will acknowledge His power and glory. For we will tell his story. When our children were blind and could not see, when they were hated and despised because of the color of their skin, and made fun of because we had no food to eat, no shoes for our feet, no clothes for our body, no love for our soul. No father to hold. No money for a doctor, no lawyer for our defense, no supreme court for our offense.

You came in the form of a man, with a magnificence plan, not to hurt no man. Healing the sick and the broken hearted. For your love makes no sense. The most undeveloped, scariest, deadliest place on earth is the human heart.

The way he viewed man and sees God. It's a gold mine waiting to be discovered, but hidden by debris and clutter. The remains of something broken down, destroyed, or an accumulation. Oh, how many times have I become fascinated with death. Seeing it as a way of being rescued from a life full of pain and suffering. Perhaps a way of escaping a world devoted to desensitized human beings as play things. But is that not the way we have done God? He is despised and rejected by men: a man of sorrows, and acquainted with grief: and we hid our faces from him: he was despised, and we esteemed him not. Who hath believed our report? And to whom is the arm of the Lord revealed? For he shall grow up before him as a tender plant, and as a root out of a dry ground: he hath no form, nor comeliness; and when we shall see him, there is no beauty that we should desire him.

Until we become a people and nation whose value system is higher than our fleshly appetites there is no end to our termination. Our comfort zone of acceptance, tolerance, friendship with ways that defeat us instead of complete us.

These four studies and directives are inspired and ordained by God to keep us focused, committed, and dedicated to the true origin of divine designed. These four studies and directives establish thoughts of love, joy, peace, kindness, and longsuffering. *"Remember now thy Creator in the days of thy youth, while the evil days come not, nor the years draw nigh, when thou shalt say; I have no pleasure in them (Ecclesiastes 12:1). Rejoice, O young man, in thy youth; and let thy heart cheer thee in the days of thy youth, and walk in the ways of thine heart, and in the sight of thine eyes: but know thou, that for all these things God will bring thee into judgment. Therefore remove sorrow from thy heart, and put away evil from thy flesh: for childhood and youth are vanity.(Ecclesiastes 11:9-10).*

And further, by these, my son, be admonished: of making many books there is no end: and much study a weariness of the flesh. Let us hear the conclusion of the whole matter: Fear God, and keep his commandments: for this is the whole duty of man. For God shall bring every work into judgment, with every secret thing, whether it be good, or whether it be evil"(Ecclesiastes 12:12-14).

CHAPTER ONE

"Be not thou envious against evil men, neither desire to be with them. For their heart studieth destruction and their lips talk of mischief" *(Proverbs 24:1-2).*

They seem to have it all—the big houses, ladies, money, fame, and fortune. The America idiot, oh, I am sorry, idol. We worship them, we adore them, and we even desire to be like them. In our search for acceptance, approval, power, provision, and dominion, we use any means necessary—lying, cheating, stealing, and killing—in order to fulfill ones desire for power. For dominion, we destroy property and sacrifice innocent lives, and the rights, privileges and freedoms of others. Two of the enemy's greatest signs and symptoms can be found in its greatest achievements; destruction and mischief. The true focus of evil men is not the desires of God but is pride and lust. This is its stigma, its trademark. The Pharaoh's attempted to secure the future, safety, and welfare of his own people, and out of a spirit of fear, decided the price was worth the lives of millions of defenseless, helpless male Hebrew children. Foolish, full of envy, strife, and every evil way, he found himself committing horrible crimes against humanity. Folly, foolishness is joy to him that is destitute of Godly wisdom. WHEN THE WICKED COMETH THEN COMETH ALSO CONTEMPT AND WITH IGNOMINY, DEEP PERSONAL HUMILIATION and DISGRACE REPROACH.

Adam's fall could have been contributed to his inability to discern the difference between good and evil or right or wrong. But if this was the case, he would have been found innocent. But he had no defense because it stated he willfully sinned. It's amazing the power of influence to be and to do evil. For it is not good to accept the person of the wicked, to overthrow the righteous in judgment. *"Envy thou not the oppressor, and choose none of his ways"* (Proverbs 3:31). *"Behold, I send you forth as sheep in the midst of wolves; be ye therefore wise as serpents, and harmless as doves"* (Matthew 10:16). God strictly prohibited us from using such knowledge, wisdom, or understanding as a form of communication between one another.

Hollywood, media, music, and television study ways to profit from our lusts, not realizing how evil destroys us and them. We have this incredible admiration, and fatal attraction for evil. We have become intoxicated by bad boys and bad girl images. We despise bad food, and bad manners, but we love bad company. In the book of Acts it is recorded that the Pharisees had gotten together to plot and plan the death of Paul. They will not sleep, eat or drink, until they destroyed a man who works were not evil, but good. *"Woe unto them that call evil good, and good evil; that put darkness for light, and light for darkness; that put bitter for sweet' and sweet for bitter!" (Isaiah 5:20).*

During the time Hitler ruled over Germany, he proclaimed and promised he would not attack Belgium or Holland. During the same time, his generals were making plans to invade both countries. I think it is foolish to trust the words of thy enemies. Remember, your enemies are not always visible. For we have been forewarned not to trust any man, only God's absolute truth. *"For it was not an enemy that reproached me; then I could have borne it: neither was it he that hated me that magnify himself against me; then I would have hid myself from him: But it was thou, a man my equal, my guide, and mine acquaintance. We took sweet counsel together, and walked unto the house of God in company"* (Psalms:55:12-14).

The brutality of the Barbarian wars demonstrates man's unwillingness to come together peacefully. They study plans on how to destroy one another. Instead of attacking evil, they became evil—walking, talking, breathing instruments of death—perfect lethal weapons of mass destruction. For the perfect strategy to overcome evil is good. These studies are driven by a different breed of man, one that is a dangerous species of mankind and a lost, dark, cruel world. And God saw that the wickedness of man was great in the earth and that every imagination of the thoughts of his heart was only evil continually; a dark reality of power, purpose and passion. Remember, the disrespect of your enemy, whose desire is to sift you as wheat. *"The enemy said, I will pursue, I will overtake, I will divide the spoil; my lust shall be satisfied upon them; I will draw my sword, my hand shall destroy them"* (Exodus 15:9).

As the four seasons change the face of the earth, these four fantastic studies, shall challenge the minds, hearts, and souls of men. *"No weapon that is formed against thee shall prosper; and every tongue that shall rise against thee in judgment thou shalt condemn. This is the heritage of the servants of the Lord, and their righteousness is of me, saith the Lord"* (Isaiah 54:17). The threat is real. We cannot and must not underestimate the cruel intentions of evil men.

They must not be tolerated, but eliminated. It's been said that there is a thousand ways to die but only one way to live. Do not enter into relationships with people who are evil. It is hazardous to your health. *"Be sober, be vigilant; because your adversary the devil, as a roaring lion, walketh about, seeking whom he may devour" (I Peter 5:8).* *"For he that will love life, and see good days, let him refrain his tongue from evil, and his lips that they speak no guile: Let him eschew evil and do good; let him seek peace and ensue it. For the eyes of the Lord are over the righteous, and his ears are open unto their prayers: but the face of the Lord is against them that do evil" (I Peter 3:10-12).* We have been told, to love our enemy. I have discovered that there are three ways to love your enemy (1). Pray for them, (2). Leave them alone, and (3). Destroy them with the word of God. Don't ignore them.

TOPIC
STUDY TO STUDY

CHAPTER ONE

"Be not thou envious against evil men, neither desire to be with them: For their heart studieth destruction and their lips talk of mischief" (Proverbs 24:1-2)

Prayer Focus and Reflections:

_____

_____

_____

_____

_____

_____

_____

_____

_____

_____

_____

_____

_____

_____

_____

_____

CHAPTER TWO

"The heart of the righteous studieth to answer: but the mouth of the wicked poureth out evil things" (**Proverbs 15:28**).

When I was a child, my parents taught me that if you don't have anything good to say about someone, then say nothing at all. So, how do you answer the nay sayers, critics, unbelievers, corrupters and skeptics. Those who come to steal, kill, and destroy your faith, dreams, and vision. These studies are easy, powerful and precise. While some come out of a genuine desire for the truth. In which case, you don't answer them equally, others do not. We are taught, to first seek the kingdom of God and his righteousness in order to establish power and purpose.

As we study the life of Jesus, he demonstrated in words, as well as deeds, how we should conduct ourselves. Because he wasn't caught off guard or surprised by the deception of man. Many times, we abort our assignment because we fail to have a clear understanding of his mission. He didn't come to condemn the world, but that it may be saved and preserved. The attitude of the heart and of the righteous, studies to answer, to help, to heal, and to discover ways and methods to bring mankind together. He intentionally studied tactics, strategies, maneuvers, and techniques to heal the broken hearted, to set the captives free, and to restore health to the sick. One of the greatest indications of the condition or contents in a person's heart is what he does (actions) and what he says (conversation). The very foundation of our faith is founded upon who and what we value, respect, love, and honor. Don't we honor and love God for his faithfulness, kindness, love, grace, and truth, none of which relies on any physical features. But we fall in and out of love with people because of how they look. The condition of our heart reveals who we are. It's been said that love is unconditional. But who and what we believe determines the condition of our heart. *"For out of the abundance of the heart the mouth speaketh" (Matthew 12:34).* Man judges by outer appearance and God judges by a man's heart. A manifestation of his behavior and conversation reveals a man's motive. Our ability to afflict pain and suffering has been effectively illustrated through our malice, guile, hypocrisies, envies, and evil speech towards one another.

We live in a world where those who are rich and famous are significant and the rest are invisible. In our world, there seems to be more problem than solutions and more questions than answers. There is a growing epidemic, disease, hopelessness, and helplessness, which leaves us defenseless against common everyday problems, situations, and circumstances, many of which are beyond our control. Some of us have found or either knows someone who has found themselves in divorce court, bankruptcies, and criminal court. A courtship with death, gloom, and destruction.

So, I ask myself, what's the use? Who's to blame? If I don't study, I fail; if I do study, I fail! So why study? What's the use! People who find themselves void of these studies are full of animosity, anxiety, and depression. They often react to issues of life with anger, bitterness, and malice. Just recently, we witnessed the private life of Tiger Woods unfold before our very eyes. What we witnessed did more damage than good. For it is written: "For the wrath of man worketh not the righteousness of God" (James 1:20). For God takes no pleasure in wickedness. When the woman was caught in the very act of adultery, man's desire was to stone her and condemn her. But Jesus' desire was to correct the sin and restore the woman's value and dignity. Our reaction towards Tiger Woods said more about our insanity than his infidelity. It revealed our idolatrous relationship with man. These types of actions predicate a guaranteed outcome full of violence, chaos, conflict, and confusion. Anything that is absent, void of that which is pure, honest, just, lovely, and of a good report finds itself incapable of producing good fruit. We have unsuitable, incompatible, undesirable, imperfect thoughts and ways. It is sad, but true; many of us neglect to seek God's Word for answers. Therefore, we suffer unnecessary losses and pain.

It is incomprehensible why we expect to have a great relationship with God when our ways and ideas are full of unrighteousness. What a wonderful way to live and learn—driven by righteousness instead of reward. "*Blessed are they which do hunger and thirst after righteousness: for they shall be filled*" *(Matthew 5:6)*. At last, fulfillment—man's final frontier. The benefits and features of God's righteousness are insurmountable. For the driven factor of Adam's and Eve's behavior was reward. They never once questioned whether it was right or wrong. "*And the scripture was fulfilled which saith, Abraham believed God, and it was imputed unto him for righteousness: and he was called the friend of God*" *(James 2:23)*. Study to answer and train a child which way he or she must go. Study to answer and to prepare those who will face foreseen and unforeseen dangers. Study to answer and, perhaps one day, you shall come up with a cure for cancer. How to bounce back, go forward, and stand still. Help us love instead of hate. Hope instead of fear. Believe instead of doubt. Pray instead of worry. *"Jesus answered and said unto him, Art thou a master of Israel, and knowest not these things?" (John 3:10).*

CHAPTER TWO

"The heart of the righteous studieth to answer: but mouth of the wicked poureth out evil things" **(Proverbs 15:28).**

Prayer Focus and Reflections:

_____

_____

_____

_____

_____

_____

_____

_____

_____

_____

_____

_____

_____

_____

_____

_____

CHAPTER THREE

"Study to shew thyself approved unto God, a workman that needeth not to be ashamed, rightly dividing the word of truth" (II Timothy 2:15).

Many times, we often fail because of our inability to rightly divide the word of truth. There are several reasons for such behavior. What maybe true for the tiger is not true for the leopard. One has spots and one has stripes. However, their different features do not change the truth of their existence. The heart, mind, soul, and spirit are all of the same body; but they are controlled, governed, and ruled by different laws. When we find ourselves under the influences of the natural man every problem and every answer becomes natural, causing man to misdiagnose, or recognize the true origin of their signs and symptoms. *"And when the tempter came to him, he said, If thou be the son of God, command that these stones be made bread. But he answered and said, It is written, Man shall not live by bread alone, but by every word that proceedeth out of the mouth of God" (Matthew 4:3-4).*

Many times, we make the mistake by fixing the effect rather than its cause. These manifestations can be seen, as a result of the imprisonment of the victim while setting the criminal free. Over 1.5 million men and women are incarcerated for violent crimes against one another. In order for such crimes to be committed, certain laws must be broken. We confuse time with change. Let me explain: While we punish the criminal, we fail to correct the crime. The system is not set up to reform, correct, or rehabilitate the criminal, but to punish. Time absent of correction equals no change. Often, a man's motives for study are not to please God but to impress man. For first impressions are lasting impressions. Sticks and stones may hurt my bones but words will never offend me. These clichés are not far from the truth. *"And lo a voice from heaven, saying, This is my beloved Son, in whom I am well pleased"(Matthew 3:17)*. The perfect example of this can be found in the Gospel of Matthew, the Pharisees' rejection of Jesus. They despised his teachings because it revealed their motives. They appeared to be men of God outwardly, but inwardly they were wolves in sheep's clothing. For they found no pleasure in Christ! So their true intentions were to use the words of the Lord to gain the trust of man, in order to profit from their wealth. *"For I say unto you, That except your righteousness shall exceed the righteousness of the scribes and Pharisees, ye shall in no case enter into the kingdom of heaven" (Matthew5:20)*. This statement facilitates a distinct difference or a clear illustration of the righteousness of man and the righteousness of God. Their shame, once exposed, misinterpreted the word of God completely to become furious and proud instead of being humbled, or corrected by the word of God. Pride would not allow them to be corrected by God; therefore, shame remained. It prohibited them from achieving two specific priorities: (1) seeking God's approval, and (2) rightly dividing the word of truth. *"Commit thy works unto the Lord and thy thoughts shall be established" (Proverbs 16:3). "Jesus answered and said unto them, This is the work of God, that ye believe on him whom he hath sent" (John 6:29). It is also written: "These were more noble than those in Thessalonica, in that they received the word with all readiness of mind, and searched the scriptures daily, whether those things were so" (Acts 17:11). "For as the body without the spirit (proof) is dead, so faith without works (proof) is dead also" (James 2:26).* These terms and conditions have been established to protect and prevent us from being deceived. The greatest assassination of a saint is his ignorance.

Once upon a time man had a great appreciation and value for life. He believed, and cherished the secrets of absolute truth. We are to be the light of the world, salt of the earth, and a manifestation of life. We have a clear motive for studying. Our true intentions are to please God and not man. A worker whose works appeals to the flesh and not the spirit should be ashamed. He seeks to please his flesh at your expense; therefore, becoming his provider or source instead of God's. The truth is always accurate. After all, who are we trying to please? Have we become people pleasers instead of God pleasers? Only you can answer the question. For we have been forewarned to be aware of false prophets; for they shall be many.

While we hate being lied to, we take pleasure in lying to others. But the preparations of the heart of man, and the answer of the tongue, are from the Lord. *"Thou shalt remember all the way which the Lord thy God led thee these forty years in the wilderness, to humble thee, and to prove thee, to know what was in thine heart, whether thou wouldest keep his commandments or no"* (Deuteronomy 8:2). *"For thou art an holy people unto the Lord thy God: the Lord thy God hath chosen thee to be a special people unto himself, above all people that are upon the face of the earth"* (Deuteronomy 7:6). *"For I know the thoughts that I think toward you, saith the Lord, thoughts of peace, and not of evil, to give you an expected end"* (Jeremiah 29:11).

One of the greatest weaknesses of man is his misguided expectation. For no man can serve two masters. For he will hate one and love the other. The problem with most of us is that we try to blend the two, which creates mental and physical disorders, for diseases are no more than outward manifestations of an inner occurrence. These signs and symptoms are patterns of behavior which have an expected end, death because they cause the body to attack or assault itself. *"And always, night and day, he was in the mountains, and in the tombs, crying, and cutting himself with stones" (Mark 5:5).* This is proof that the condition of the body can be found in the mind. *"Why should ye be stricken any more? Ye will revolt more and more: the whole head is sick, and the whole heart faint. From the sole of the foot even unto the head there is no soundness in it; but wounds, and bruises, and putrefying sores: they have not been closed, neither bound up, neither mollified with ointment" (Isaiah 1:5-6).*

Evidence is the effects, not the cause. It is a sick, confused individual who indulges in attitudes, behaviors, and conducts that go against the principles of God, with expectation of honor and respect. Our obedience builds an impenetrable fortress against biological, psychological, and physiological warfare. God has given us specific protocol which defiles all laws of physics and the practice or profession of medicine. For which medicine did Jesus use to heal the lepers, the woman with the issue of blood, or the blind? I don't condemn medicine, nor do I condemn the power of God. When something is not rightly divided, it creates confusion, doubt, and suspicions. Causing one to become susceptible to being easily influenced, manipulated, and controlled by fear instead of being governed by wisdom.

TOPIC
STUDY TO STUDY

CHAPTER THREE

"Study to shew thyself approved unto God, a workman that needeth not to be ashamed, rightly dividing the word of truth" (II Timothy 2:15).

Prayer Focus and Reflections:

_____

_____

_____

_____

_____

_____

_____

_____

_____

_____

_____

_____

_____

_____

_____

_____

CHAPTER FOUR

"And that ye study to be quiet, and to do your own business, and work with your own hands, as we commanded you" **(I Thessalonians 4:11).**

How often do we error in judgment because we hear without thinking or listening to what is truly being said. We are quick to speak and slow to hear. We become emotional creatures, driven by our senses full of rage, anger, selfishness, and madness. Feelings that cause us to become dominated rulers of evil, instead of saints of God. *"The words of wise men are heard in quiet more than the cry of him that ruleth among fools" (Ecclesiastes 9:17).* The consequences of being a poor listener can be found in the grave and prison; therefore, becoming a foreigner or stranger in the sight of God and a fool in the sight of man. Nevertheless, there is a time to keep silent and a time to speak. King Saul, the first ruler, over Israel refused to listen to the commandments of God. Becoming a landlord of the dead instead of a servant of the living. How can one learn or experience the ways of God, if he rejects his instructions. The power, position, and purpose of a King is to provide provision, protection, and to help nourish your body, mind, soul, and spirit. The quality of our lives should be *"the hidden man of the heart, in that which is* not corruptible, even the ornament of a meek and quiet spirit which is in the sight of God of great price" (I Peter 3:4).

When I was a child it was said that an empty wagon makes a lot of noise. "These are murmurers, complainers, walking after their own lusts; and their mouth speaketh great swelling words, having men's persons in admiration because of advantage" (Jude 1:16). We often allow our mission to be ambushed or sabotaged by the interferences and opinion of others. "But let none of you suffer as a murderer, or as a thief, or as an evildoer, or as a busybody in other men's matters" (I Peter 4:15). For we hear that there are some which walk among you disorderly, working not at all, but are busybodies. And withal they learn to be idle, wandering about from house to house and not only idle but tattlers also and busybodies speaking things they ought not. Let us learn from Jesus, busy about our father's business. Let us not be accused, "Ye are of your father the devil, and the lusts of your father ye will do. He was a murderer from the beginning, and abode not in the truth, because there is no truth in him. When he speaketh a lie, he speaketh of his own: for he is a liar and the father of it. And because I (Jesus) tell you the truth ye believe me not" (John 8:44-45). Do we not set ourselves up by relying on others for information?

When Joseph discovered Mary with child, it was critical that he kept quiet about it to protect God's secret and to guard the lives of Mary and Jesus. The future of the world was in his hands. "Better is an handful with quietness, than both the hands full with travail and vexation of spirit" (Ecclesiastes 4:6). Can God trust you to keep quiet? Because we live in a tell-all society, exposing people's most embarrassing moments. Not once considering the damage, pain, and suffering it may cause one family's reputation or friends. There are certain conversations between God, doctor, and lawyer which are confidential. Discretion and good judgment use to be very important ingredients in a person's character. You have the right to remain silent: anything you say can and will be used against you in the court of law. You have a right to an attorney. If you can't afford one: one will be appointed to you. In time of war being quiet becomes a matter of life or death! *"And the men answered her, Our life for yours, if ye utter not this our business. And it shall be, when the Lord hath given us the land, that we will deal kindly and truly with thee" (Joshua 2:14).* A code or oath of silence is the key factor, the strength or weakness of any organization.

In order to maintain a perfect balance between when to talk and not to, we must have a clear understanding of the power of speech. *"Death and life are in the power of the tongue: and they that love it shall eat the fruit thereof"* (Proverbs 18:21). "Whoso keepeth his mouth and his tongue, keepeth his soul from troubles" (Proverbs 21:23). *"Even so the tongue is a little member, and boasteth great things. Behold, how great a matter a little fire kindleth. And the tongue is a fire, a world of iniquity: so is the tongue among our members, that it defileth the whole body, and setteth on fire the course of nature; and it is set on fire of hell.* But the tongue can no man tame; it is an unruly evil, full of deadly poison" (James 3:5-6,8). Many of us have faith without works, and prayer without actions. We believe God, but do not take the necessary steps to combat or correct the situation. We hear the word but do not obey; therefore, forfeiting the benefits and promises of God. These false balances create the perfect profile of a person who lacks the skills, wisdom, understanding, and knowledge to obtain the self control needed.

We must cease from instruction or any instructor who teaches us half truths. *"Cease, my son, to hear the instruction that causeth to err from the words of knowledge"*

(Proverbs: 19:27.) For everyone that useth milk is unskilful in the word of righteousness: for he is a babe. But strong meat belongeth to them that are of full age, even those who by reason of use have their senses exercised to discern both good and evil" (Hebrews: 5:13-14). Imagine your life with these studies and imagine your life without them. These four studies have the abilities to change the species of man, into a new creature, from a savage, unintelligent beast into a wise, compassionate being. The wisdom of God passeth all understanding. Life begins with a choice. So therefore chose wisely. Your final destination depends on it. *"But whoso hearkeneth unto me shall dwell safely, and shall be quiet from fear of evil" (Proverbs 1:33). "Seeing then that these things cannot be spoken against, ye ought to be quiet, and to do nothing rashly" (Acts 19:36)*. Interruption and distraction causes more misunderstanding, conflicts, chaos, and confusion than we can count. There are many ways and reasons to avoid unnecessary obstacles. Being quiet helps us discern whether a matter is worthy to speak on. For there is a diffence between those who are seeking answers and those who are seeking trouble. *"Open thy mouth for the dumb in the cause of all such as are appointed to destruction. Open thy mouth, judge righteously, and plead the cause of the poor and needy" (Proverbs 31:8-9)*.

For a long time, people kept quiet about the conditions of the dumb, poor, and needy. The shame, despair, hopelessness, helplessness, and homelessness caused man to turn his back on his fellow man. This created the perfect storm for violence, corruption, death, and destruction. Brought on by a conflict of interest, there was a voice born, whose words sent messages of controversy. A kingdom not of this world. A government not ruled by the people, but by a righteousness above, and beyond mankind. Jesus, a man of peace.

CHAPTER FOUR

"And that ye study to be quiet, and to do your own business, and work with your own hands, as we commanded you" (I Thessalonians 4:11).

Prayer Focus and Reflections:

_____
_____
_____
_____
_____
_____
_____
_____
_____
_____
_____
_____
_____
_____
_____
_____

CHAPTER FIVE

DIRECTIVES

"In all thy ways acknowledge him, and he shall direct thy paths." (Proverbs 3:6).

Since the beginning of time, God has always been deeply concerned about the welfare of his people. *"Ye are my witnesses, saith the Lord, and my servant whom I have chosen: that ye may know and believe me, and understand that I am he: Before me there was no God formed, neither shall there be after me. I, even I, am the Lord; and beside me there is no savior"* (Isaiah 43:10-11). We live in a world, full of misguided trust, pride, lust, greed, and extortion. Our leader's directives serve to guide or influence the power or conscience of our being but it has been replaced or misplaced with an entirely new agenda. Changes once considered a disgraceful act against God, now, we welcome it with open arms. *"And Jesus went into the temple of God, and cast out all them that sold and bought in the temple, and overthrew the tables of the money changers and the seats of them that sold doves. And said unto them, It is written, My house shall be called the house of prayer; but ye have made it a den of thieves"* (Matthew 21:12-13).

One of the greatest temptations or weaknesses of man is to become wealthy at the expense others. *"For what does it profit a man to gain the whole world and lose his soul"* (Mark 8:36). We have witnessed how such behavior has destroyed the world. So why would we follow such a weak, wicked system?

There are four directives, motives for these studies. They can be found in II Timothy 3:16-17, *"All scripture is given by inspiration of God, and is profitable for doctrine, for reproof, for correction, for instruction in righteousness."* Reason: That the man of God maybe perfect: thoroughly furnished unto all good works. Our God is an awesome God. He prepares his leaders, on how and what to teach; providing us with proof, evidence, signs, and wonders that no man can dispute. God's relationship with us is honest, instead of being critical or condemning. He finds ways of correction and instructions in righteousness. *"Blessed is the man that walketh not in the counsel of the ungodly, nor standeth in the way of sinners, nor sitteth in the seat of the scornful"* (Psalms 1:1). Mix messages, mix agendas, mix signals, and crazy priorities are only a few misguided reasons that cause man to become chaotic. *"The kings of the earth set themselves, and the rulers take counsel together, against the Lord, and against his anointed"* (Psalms 2:2). These four directives are designed to protect and to prevent us from becoming entangled in such nonsense, by educating us God's way.

The first directive we shall examine is doctrine. The word doctrine is defined as a principle or position in a branch of knowledge or system of belief. *"Behold, I have taught you statutes, and judgments, even as the Lord my God commanded me, that ye should do so in the land whither ye go to possess it. Keep therefore and do them; for this is your wis-*

dom and your understanding in the sight of the nations, which shall hear all these statutes, and say, Surely this great nation is a wise and understanding people" (Deuteronomy 4:5-6). We are a nation within a nation. We have been fore-warned, *"no man that warreth entangleth himself with affairs of this life; that he may please him who hath chosen him to be a soldier" (II Timothy 2:4).* The world in its attempt to please the people found themselves in contempt with God. The future of mankind can be determined by who and what we trust. Going about to establish their own righteousness they have chosen their own death. *"There is a way that seemeth right unto a man, but the end thereof are the ways of death"* (Proverbs 14:12). God is not the author of confusion, then who is? The ways of man is full of strife, envy, conflict, and confusion. His focus is on things that have nothing to do with life. Driven by insecurities, he begins to create and design new inventions to make things better only to find them illogical and irresponsibly worst. So who is teaching our children? What are our children being taught? Traditionally, according to the standards of man we go to church every Sunday or Saturday singing, praising, and giv-ing ten percent of our income in the name of the Lord. In exchange, we are taught that God will reward you by giving you double for your troubles. A relationship built on nickels, dimes, pennies, quarters, and dollars. *"This people draweth nigh unto me with their mouth, and honoreth me with their lips; but their heart is far from me. But in vain they do wor-ship me, teaching for doctrines the commandments of men"* (Matthew 15:8-9). It's been said, "I think if you study—if you lean too much of what other have done, you may tend to take the same direction as everybody else" (Jim Henson). These studies and directives challenge us to think, teach, and reach higher than traditionally.

TOPIC
STUDY TO STUDY

CHAPTER FIVE

"In all thy ways acknowledge him, and he shall direct thy paths." (Proverbs 3:6).

Prayer Focus and Reflections:

_____

_____

_____

_____

_____

_____

_____

_____

_____

_____

_____

_____

_____

_____

_____

_____

CHAPTER SIX

REPROOF

"To whom also he showed himself alive after his passion by many infallible proofs, being seen of them forty days, and speaking of the things pertaining to the kingdom of God" (Acts 1:3).

The word *proof* is defined as evidence of truth. *Reproof* is defined as censure for a fault. It is written: *"The simple believeth every word: but the prudent man looketh well to his going"* (Proverbs 14:15). When I was a child we were taught not to question God. This very statement contradicts such a belief. *"Beloved, believe not every spirit, but try the spirits whether they are of God: because many false prophets are gone out into the world"* (I John 4:1). How often do we receive information without verifying it? We don't check or test for accuracy to confirm our information to be true or not. So, in the end, we often find ourselves suffering great loss and embarrassment. Many battles have been defeated, many lives destroyed, only because no one took the initiative to check it out. False Prophets love such people. When we take our clothes to the cleaners we expect for them to be 100% clean. When we take our car to the shop we expect everything to be done 100% right. When we get our pay checks, we expect it to be 100% accurate. But with the word of God, our expectations change. We settle for half truths, and whole lies. We accept false teachings as a way of truth. Everything else has high priority, expectation, or value. A man can tell you anything and you believe it, never once questioning it for accuracy or authenticity and becoming an easy target for such nonsense. This type of life style is full of insanity.

We are taught not to trust any man, yet we do. The consequences are devastating; suicides, homicides, violence, and extortion just to name a few of its devices. There is definitely a disastrous plan or connection concerning such proof. As art imitates life, there is an infallible truth between God and man. Once he can trust and is dependent upon, for it's been tried, proven and tested. We live in a world at an accelerated rate. We are putting our trust more and more in the hands of others, and less and less in our own. We are becoming machines and brain washed zombies, who are controlled by the values, thoughts and opinions of others. *"And Elijah came unto all the people, and said, How long halt ye between two opinions? If the Lord be God, follow him: but if Baal, then follow him. And the people answered him not a word"(I Kings 18:21).* It is these types of behaviors which restrict access to the kingdom of God. For a double minded man is unstable in all of his ways. The word of God is priceless, yet we handle it in such a reckless way. This is your life, choose, this day, the God you want to serve. The more we study and learn about God; the more we learn about who we are. This directive is designed to identify, attack, and eliminate, all doubt. The error-proof test has revealed that it is not God who is at fault but man. *"God is not a man, that he should lie; neither the*

48

son of man, that he should repent: hath he said, and shall he not do it? Or hath he spoken, and shall he not make it good? (Numbers 23:19). But yet, it is written: *"For the time will come when they will not endure sound doctrine; but after their own lusts shall they heap to themselves teachers, having itching ears; And they shall turn away their ears from the truth, and shall be turn unto fables" (II Timothy 4:3-4).* We live in a world where lust, greed, love of money, and pride has become our God and value system.

Influenced by a manslaughter or massacre so sophisticated, it comes in the name of progress. Woe unto them that is wise in their own eyes. An invasion armed by an intruder whose terrorist attacks are within. A legacy of lies and deterioration that is devoted to ambush the whole wide world. The higher the influence; the greater the impact. *"For we wrestle not against flesh and blood, but against principalities, against powers, against the rulers of the darkness of this world, against spiritual wickedness in high places" (Ephesians 6:12).* We have come face to face with the enemy, for we are not strangers. Unless, we confront, challenge, and correct these attitudes, behaviors and conducts, we shall find ourselves in alliance with the enemy. Henceforth, becoming part of God's extermination plan. *"For if God spared not the angels that sinned, but cast them down to hell, and delivered them into chains of darkness, to be reserved unto judgment"(II Peter 2:4).* What more shall he do unto us? Let us not become infatuated with ourselves. We must correct, change, confront, challenge, and overcome the negative appetites that destroy us. For God has not given us a spirit (image) of fear, but of love, power and a sound mind. Let us walk in the spirit and not fulfill the lust of the flesh. We should observe these areas daily within ourselves, in God, and in others.

CHAPTER SIX

"To whom also he showed himself alive after his passion by many infallible proofs, being seen of them forty days, and speaking of the things pertaining to the kingdom of God" (Acts 1:3).

Prayer Focus and Reflections:

_____

_____

_____

_____

_____

_____

_____

_____

_____

_____

_____

_____

_____

_____

_____

CHAPTER SEVEN

CORRECTION

"But he (Jesus) turned, and said unto Peter, Get thee behind me, Satan: thou art an offense unto me: for thou savorest not the things that be of God, but those that be of men" (Matthew16:23).

We often attack the person instead of the problem and place blame instead of addressing the real issues. Criticizing and judging one another does not solve problems. When you love someone, you do not see their weaknesses as an opportunity to destroy them. You are to help them overcome their weakness. *"Hatred stirreth up strifes: but loveth covereth all sins"* (Proverbs 10:12). The way we handle problems can predict a healthy or unhealthy outcome. We know that, *"correction is grievous unto him that forsaketh the way; and he that hateth reproof shall die"* (Proverbs 15:10). Man's ways limits and interferes with the plans of God. *"Yea, they turned back and tempted God, and limited the Holy One of Israel"* (Psalms 78:41). Man's goals have never been on God's agenda. The ways of God creates environments, atmospheres, and conditions to grow and develop relationships that strengthen the mind, body, heart, and soul.

51

When Jesus entered a village, it was his intention to help the poor, to set the captives free, to heal the broken hearted, to preach the good news to the oppressed, to correct, to teach, to instruct, and prove the ways of God.

The greatest foundation for change is wiliness to be corrected. We spend too much time in damage control rather than moving forward. We seem to always need to be fixed. Rehabilitation has become a permanent way of life for some. A poisonous paradise sustained by an equally dangerous relationship assassinated by a dysfunctional society. We live at a level of existence that keeps us physically strong but mentally and spiritually weak. The spirit is willing, but the flesh is weak, especially when we allow ourselves to be led, and fed by leaders, who are inexperienced in spiritual matters. We find ourselves adopting their ways. Correction has a biography that is so brilliant that it has unmistakably changed the world. When mankind finds himself living in very uncomfortable or unsatisfactory conditions, he begins to resist inconvenience as a form of happiness. Therefore, making the necessary corrections to create and establish a better world. But he forgot the true anatomy of correction and that is truth and mercy. We cannot, and must not underestimate the dangerous consequences of correction without mercy and truth. It can cause one to act abusive towards oneself as well as others. *"By mercy and truth iniquity is purged: and by the fear of the Lord men depart from evil" (Proverbs 16:6).* Truth without mercy is brutal; mercy without truth is suicidal; therefore, sacrificing a true chance of hope and redemption to that of a counterfeit lifestyle that doesn't exist. One of the patterns of a wise man is his love for correction.

CHAPTER SEVEN

"But he (Jesus) turned, and said unto Peter, Get thee behind me, Satan: thou art an offense unto me: for thou savorest not the things that be of God, but those that be of men" (Matthew16:23).

Prayer Focus and Reflections:

_____

_____

_____

_____

_____

_____

_____

_____

_____

_____

_____

_____

_____

_____

_____

_____

CHAPTER EIGHT

"And the work of righteousness shall be peace; and the effect of righteousness quietness and assurance for ever" (Isaiah 32:17).

INSTRUCTION IN RIGHTEOUSNESS

In the beginning, God gave man several plain and simple instructions. Since then, because of sin many more instructions have been added. God's instructions are messages of hope that produce life. Everything we buy and sell comes with instructions. Imagine a world without them. We would be totally lost. It is not a lack of intelligence, but lack of obedience which has put mankind in harms way. We should devote ourselves to that which is holy, and despise that which is evil. For the lord takes no pleasure in wickedness.

In the New Testament, we are instructed to *"seek ye first the kingdom of God, and his righteousness; and all these things shall be added unto you"* (Matthew 6:33). But instead, we seek fame and fortune and a reputation. God has made an agreement, or covenant, with man. *"And the scripture was fulfilled which saith, Abraham believed God, and it was imputed unto him for righteousness and he was called the Friend of God"* (James 2:23). The righteousness of man is not the same as for God. Why? Man is moved by situations and circumstances, and we make decisions based on feelings and emotions. The Lord does not have respect of person. His ways do not discriminate against any man based on race, gender, height, weight, or fortune. Many of which are self inflicted or unpredictable, yet predictable reactions. *"But we are all as an unclean thing, and all our righteousness are as filthy rags: and we all do fade as a leaf; and our iniquities, like the wind, have taken us away" (Isaiah 64:6).* A covenant, agreement with death. We live in houses we did not build. We eat food that we did not grow. We wear clothes we did not make. We read books we did not write. How hard could it be? We make life hard because we refuse to follow God's instruction. *"In the way of right-eousness is life; and in the pathway thereof, there is no death" (Proverbs 12:28).* So what is our alternative? *'Poverty and shame shall be to him that refuseth instruc-tion: but he that regardeth reproof shall be honoured" (Proverbs 13:18).* In the beginning, God gave man two instructions concerning which tree to eat from. In an instant man went from being the king of the world to the scum of the earth. For whatsoever a man thinketh (believeth) in his heart so is he! We have been infiltrated by a belief system that doesn't protect us against virus and other security risk designed to destroy us. Instead of protecting our immune system, we expose it to all types of diseases.

The survival of our species, is founded in the nucleus of these studies and directives. For they are the very DNA that is missing in our genetic make up. We have teachers who have no honor or respect for the things of God. We have mayors and governors who have no fear of God. And you wonder why our world is so messed up. Making laws that are contrary to the laws of God. *"In those days there was no king in Israel, but every man did that which was right in his own eyes" (Judges 17:6).* All the ways of a man are clean in his or her own eyes: but the Lord weigheth the spirits. If we lived in a world absent of all law and order, it would be the perfect condition to annihilate mankind. Slavery was such a place, where the privileges of a few were gained at the expense of so many. Today, we have companies that are making an outrages amount of profits, and the top executives making millions, but, many of their employees are barely making it. Mans' way of establishing his own form of government. For Man's righteousness does not produce the righteousness of the Almighty God.

CHAPTER EIGHT

"And the work of righteousness shall be peace; and the effect of righteousness quietness and assurance for ever" (Isaiah 32:17).

Prayer Focus and Reflections:

_____

_____

_____

_____

_____

_____

_____

_____

_____

_____

_____

_____

_____

_____

_____

_____

_____

SUMMARY

We are born into a world, culture, or society that teaches us from birth to study to prove our intelligence, in exchange for rewards, acceptance and approval. This type of thinking implies that we are dumb, unintelligent, and stupid beings. Driven by a set of standards, belief, rules and regulations that turns mankind against one another. A system so evil, diabolically devoted to studies designed to create an image of godliness. An artificial intelligence causing mankind to commit genocide against his own species. The fruit of the righteous is a tree of life: and he that winneth souls is wise. For there is nothing, no one more valuable than the human soul!

In the Bible there are four specific, distinct studies that are intentionally designed to confront and overcome these counterfeit attempts to cancel or reverse the image of GOD. For who would ever think through omission, that the educational system would commit such a crime against humanity? For many have a zeal for God but not according to knowledge. In our schools there is a strong presence of misconduct, violence, conflict, strife, disrespect for authority, murder, suicide, and confusion. Because of the world's hatred towards God's way, their children are being cursed. These negative images are often viewed as a defense to confront, or combat offensive behaviors for protection. There is a great need for education reform. For there is a very vital, irreplaceable, important ingredient missing. Children are an easy target for the cruel reality of a world gone mad without God. No matter how we cut it, shape it, slice it, or dice it. Nothing, no one can take the place of the one wise, true, and living God. Each generation's concerns and complaints seem to be the same. Health care reform, education, poverty, and crime, but these are no more than signs of no respect and honor nor the courage to do that which is right.

God foresaw that there would be assaults and attacks against our faith. For what we believe is no religion, but a way of life. When we reject God, our life becomes a death sentence so severe, an injustice so cruel, a worship so evil until it sounds more like a science fiction movie instead of a scheme to destroy and kill mankind. As a deterrent, we put our children into uniforms and find them still uninformed concerning the truth. Yet, we witness the evidence, proof of its existence each and everyday, as we sit comfortably in our homes. Our children are being slaughtered, massacred, assassinated, like sheep in a war which seems to have no end or meaning. In our own country, we fight against rape, robbery, and murder. And we fight for power, property, and possession at the alienation or expense of others, violating their rights and privileges while losing one's own. *"Thy princes are rebellious and companions of thieves: everyone loveth gifts and followeth after rewards: they judge not the fatherless, neither doth the cause of the widow come unto them" (Isaiah 1:23).*

The world would have us believe that we have need for knowledge to be poured into us. GOD teaches that we already have it. *"It is written in the prophets, And they shall be all taught of God. Every man therefore that hath heard, and hath learned of the Father, cometh unto me" (John 6:45).* Perhaps this is the great debate. That we are made in the image of the most intelligent being known to man. Entirely lacking nothing. For it is he who has made us and not we ourselves. But imagine for one moment creating a people and the world and not being invited to be part of it. The god of this world has systematically implemented a habitation that breeds contempt, corruption, and destroys the human race. It's called the heart! Where are our fathers, do they not exist? Where are our mothers, in search of survival? So where is God, just where man has put him, in a worldly system where he doesn't exist! We have camouflaged and disguised the truth with Santa Clause and the Easter Bunny. Aimed to belittle, it is devaluing the true image of God. No other holiday has duel purposes. A little leaven, poison (error) lumps the whole lump. May the Lord have mercy on us all!

There is a systematic error in judgment, an error in data that is due to the method of measurement or observation and not due to chance. These four studies and directives paint a portrait of a people and nation driven by a love so powerful, with a commitment so great, a devotion so deep, and a mind and heart so made up; an incorruptible foundation, established by God of fearing men and women who can not be bought or sold. A kingdom where GOD'S laws rule. A nation where his people called by his name governs the land. A country where the righteousness of GOD is loved, honored, and respected. Instead of subduing the land we have allowed ourselves to be seduced and reduced. Instead of having dominion, we have allowed ourselves to become dominated by fear and unbelief. And the list goes on and on. *"Ever learning, and never able to come to the knowledge of the truth"* (II Timothy 3:7).